SHMOOZE

A Guide to Thought-Provoking Discussions
on Essential Jew

D1055824

Compiled by
Nechemia Coopersmith

Aish
HaTorah
aish.com

TARGUM/FELDHEIM

First published 2001
ISBN 0-56871-294-4
Copyright © 2001 Nechemia Coopersmith, Aish HaTorah

Comments, questions, and bulk orders can be sent to shmooze@aish.com.

Published by:
TARGUM PRESS
22700 W. 11 Mile Rd.
Southfield, MI 48034
targum@netvision.net.il
Fax: (888)298-9992
In conjunction with Aish HaTorah

Distributed by:
FELDHEIM PUBLISHERS INC.
200 Airport Executive Park
Nanuet, NY 10952
www.feldheim.com

Printed in Israel

CONTENTS

INTRODUCTION

One evening I was reading my five-year-old daughter a story when she looked up at me and asked, "Abba, why do I want to do bad things sometimes?"

Great question! I thought to myself, quickly followed by a panicky, *What do I tell her?* With my daughter eagerly waiting for a response, her bright eyes fixed on mine, I knew I had to give her some kind of sensible reply. It is no simple matter, I discovered, discussing man's drive for evil with a five-year-old.

My daughter was demonstrating the power of a good question. They pierce through our layers of intellectual malaise and shake our assumptions. They challenge us to think, explore and reach greater clarity. Good questions can also make us uncomfortable. It's a lot easier to brush them aside and duck the issue.

All too often we prefer to leave our moral furniture intact rather than reexamine where we have placed our values.

For children, however, asking questions is natural and spontaneous. No one teaches kids to seek understanding. It's as we get older, after being told repeatedly to give up looking for answers, that we learn to stop asking questions. The innate desire for knowledge needs to be nurtured and encouraged, not snuffed out by the resistance to inquire and reconsider.

This small book is first and foremost about provocative questions. Jews are "the people of the Book," and half of that book's pages are filled with questions. For thousands of years the Jewish people have been challenging, debating, arguing, refuting, probing *everything* — from the nature of God to the details of a cow's esophagus. The Torah deals with every issue under the sun. "Delve in it, delve in it! For everything is in it" (*Ethics of the Fathers 5:26*).

According to Jewish folklore, a good question is half the answer. A question carves out an inner vacuum that creates a yearning for knowledge. An answer to an unasked question is usually irrelevant.

The goal of *Shmooze* is to spark meaningful discussion on a wide range of topics. Jews from all backgrounds and ages have been using these discussion questions to provoke debate across campuses, at dinner tables, meetings and family get-togethers. These thought-provoking questions are guaranteed to add some pizzazz to your conversation with friends, family and coworkers.

Shmooze is not only about questions; it's also about answers. Each question has a brief essay that explores Judaism's approach to the issue and shares some of the relevance and depth of Jewish wisdom.

The spirit of *Shmooze* should be fun and stimulating. If you are leading a group discussion, try not to direct the conversation too much. You're not out to win an argument, nor is it your job to answer every question that arises. Your goal is to engage people in meaningful discussion and get them to listen to each other. Stir up some controversy. And don't let people just state their opinion; ask them to explain *why* they think so. Most important, have a great time!

I hope you have as much meaningful fun with *Shmooze* as I had compiling it.

Happy Shmoozing!
Nechemia Coopersmith

ACKNOWLEDGMENTS

Many people have left their indelible imprints on this small book. My *rosh yeshivah*, Rabbi Noach Weinberg, founder and dean of Aish HaTorah, taught me — and countless others — most of the ideas discussed in *Shmooze*. His keen vision, depth of insight and tireless efforts have made an incalculable impact on the Jewish people.

I would like to thank the following people for their significant input and creative ideas: my brother, Rabbi Eric Coopersmith, Rabbi Steve Baars, Rabbi Nachum Braverman, Rabbi Shimon Apisdorf, Rabbi Gershon Unger, Rabbi Dovid Geffen, Rabbi Yaakov Palatnik, Rabbi Yitzchak Berkowitz and Rabbi Noach Orlowek.

I want to express my appreciation to the dedicated staff and participants of the Jerusalem Fellowships program, who debated many of these questions and experimented with them on campuses.

My thanks go to an incredible cadre of editors who lent their much-needed skills throughout the *Shmooze* evolutionary process: Uriela Obst, Esther Greer and Shoshana Lepon. I would also like to thank Suri Brand and the professional staff at Targum Press.

At Aish HaTorah, I am fortunate to work with a tremendously talented group of graphic designers, two of whom designed the book and its cover: Yitzchak Attias and Shmuel Kaffe.

Acharonah acharonah chavivah… My dear wife, Dina, for her incisive feedback, good judgment and constant support.

1

LOVE

SHMOOZE

LOVE
QUESTIONS

1. Can you love obnoxious people?

2. How can you tell the difference beween love and infatuation?

1. LOVING OBNOXIOUS PEOPLE

A child could be an absolute terror.

He could spit on his parents, throw cereal in their faces, scribble on the walls — and they'll still love him! If you were to tell them that their son is an uncontrollable menace, chances are they would say, "Uncontrollable? Our son is just energetic! He's developing a dynamic and creative personality."

Most parents love their children no matter how obnoxious they are. Why? Because they focus on the good in their children. That is the secret to love.

A Jewish definition of love could be "the pleasure one experiences when recognizing the virtues of another person and identifying that person with those virtues."

In Jewish thought, love is an obligation. The Torah says, "Love your neighbor like yourself" (*Leviticus 19:18*). How can the Torah command an emotion? You either feel it or you don't.

Love is not a stroke of fate, a passing mood you accidentally fall into (and just as easily fall out of). It is a result of the effort you put into appreciating another person's virtues. Love is a choice. Focus on the inner beauty of another, and you will begin to love him. Focus on his flaws, and you will dislike him. Since love is an action that is within our hands, it can be commanded.

We know we should love our brothers and sisters no matter how obnoxious they can be. We do it by seeing past the negative and recognizing their inner strengths. If we extend this process outside the family, where it doesn't come so naturally, we can learn to love anyone.

The key to loving people is getting to know their virtues. The better we know someone's virtues, the better we can love and appreciate who they are. To become a loving person, become a connoisseur of people. Learn to identify their qualities. That guy you find so obnoxious? List twenty positive things you see in him. Make lists for all your friends. It's worth the effort.

IN SUMMARY

〜Love is the pleasure one experiences when recognizing the inner beauty of another person.

〜Love is not an accident. It is a choice that is within your power. Focus on another's virtues; you'll love him. Focus on his flaws; you'll dislike him.

〜Appreciate a person's virtues and make an effort to look past his faults. You'll discover you can love even the most obnoxious person.

2. LOVE VERSUS INFATUATION

What is the difference between love and infatuation?

Infatuation is "We spent the day together and it was so wonderful, and as evening came with the sun in her hair I knew this would last forever." They'll be lucky if they're speaking by next week. Infatuation rarely lasts.

Infatuation has a lot to do with desire and very little to do with genuine recognition of who the person is.

Woody Allen, in *Play It Again, Sam*, tries to pick up a girl at the Museum of Modern Art. She's viewing a Jackson Pollack painting.

Allen: What does it say to you?

Girl: Negativeness of the universe. Hideous, lonely emptiness of existence. Nothingness, the predicament of man forced to live in a barren eternity. An immense void with nothing but waste, horror and degradation in a bleak, absurd cosmos.

Allen: What are you doing Saturday night?

Girl: Committing suicide.

Allen: How about Friday night?

Woody isn't in love; he's infatuated. He's not interested in who this woman is; he's enamored with her looks. He's not listening to a word she is saying.

Love comes from a genuine appreciation of another's character. When we see someone's beauty, virtue and strength of character, it leads to love. You can't truly love someone until you know him. Saying you're in love with someone you don't truly know is like saying you love a book you haven't read. All you love is the outer jacket.

Infatuation comes and goes. A bad hair day can spell the end of a relationship. Infatuation stems from one's inner desires and has nothing to do with who the person really is. Some of the common infatuation-causers are looks, money, lifestyle, power, career and reputation. These things may attract us to the relationship, but ultimately they distract us from the person. That's why many "fall" for people they eventually find are completely wrong for them.

When your motivation for dating someone is infatuation, you are no longer dating the person — you're dating his or her looks, job and possessions. As soon as you meet someone more attractive, successful or wealthy, the relationship is over.

Only when love is built on true appreciation can it last.

How can you tell the difference between love and infatuation? If you ever catch yourself saying, "S/he's perfect!" beware! You're infatuated. Love isn't blind; infatuation is. Love is a magnifying glass.

Chances are the person who loves you more than anyone else is the one who knows your faults better than anyone else.

IN SUMMARY

~ Love is built on the appreciation of who the person truly is and is therefore lasting.

~ Infatuation stems from one's own desires (looks, money, reputation, power) and has nothing to do with who the person truly is and therefore passes.

~ Litmus test: "S/he's perfect!" Love isn't blind; infatuation is. Love is a magnifying glass. The person who loves you more than anyone else is probably the one who knows your faults better than anyone else.

BACKGROUND SOURCES

1. One does not love God except with the knowledge one has of Him. The love is commensurate with the knowledge. If there is little of it [the knowledge], there is little [love]; if there is a lot, there is a lot of love.

Maimonides, Mishnah Torah, Laws of Repentance 10:6

2. We love, says the Vilna Gaon, because we recognize noble qualities in someone.... But man's egotism makes such recognition hard to come by. We spend too much of our lives fantasizing about how beautiful, intelligent and important we are while convincing ourselves how ugly, unintelligent and unimportant others are. Our jealousy makes it difficult for us to acknowledge that another person possesses a superior quality that we lack.

Rabbi Aharon Feldman,
The River, the Kettle and the Bird, p. 143

3. God relates to the individual according to the manner with which the person relates to others.

Babylonian Talmud, Megillah 12b

4. If one were only to reflect that a person comes to love the one to whom he gives, he would realize that the only reason the other person seems a stranger to him is because he has not yet given to him; he has not taken the trouble to show him friendly concern. If I give to someone, I feel close to him; I have a share in his being. It follows that if I were to start bestowing good upon everyone I come into contact with, I would soon feel that they are all my relatives, all my loved ones. I now have a share in them all; my being has extended into all of them....

"You shall love your neighbor as yourself".... By giving to him of yourself, you will find in your soul that you and he are indeed one; you will feel in the clearest possible manner that he really is to you "as yourself."

Rabbi Eliyahu Dessler, Michtav MeEliyahu,
Discourse on Lovingkindness

5. Rabbi Leib Chasman, famous ethicist and spiritual supervisor of Chevron Yeshivah, once saw a student eating fish with great relish. "Tell me, young man," he asked him, "do you love fish?"

The student answered in the affirmative.

"If you love fish," replied Reb Leib, "then you should have cared for the one on your plate. You should have fed it and tried to make it happy. Instead you are devouring it." As the student groped for a proper response, Reb Leib explained, "Obviously you don't love fish. You love yourself!"

Rabbi Aharon Feldman,
The River, the Kettle and the Bird, p. 26

2

THE VALUE OF LIFE

SHMOOZE

THE VALUE
OF LIFE
QUESTIONS

1a. Would you be willing to murder one innocent person if it would guarantee the cure for cancer?

b. What if that one innocent person were ninety years old?

WHOSE LIFE?

Life is precious.
Any decision must reflect
its infinite value.

Let's be practical. By murdering one person, you save millions of lives. By sparing him, you save only one person — one ninety-year-old person who has already lived out the prime years of his life. In this instance, taking one life saves millions. If we value life, surely this is the right decision.

Yet most of us know intuitively that this can't be right. It's wrong to murder an innocent ninety-year-old, even if it would guarantee the cure for cancer.

Can you explain *why*?

Unfortunately this dilemma is not just theoretical. In the book *Holocaust and Halachah*, a concentration camp inmate asked a rabbi the following question:

> *The Nazis have imprisoned a hundred children whom they*

plan to murder tomorrow morning. My son is among them. I can bribe the guard to free my son, but if I do, the Nazis will grab someone else's son to replace mine. Rabbi, may I bribe the guards to free him?

The rabbi refused to answer. From his silence, the father derived the rabbi's answer — he was forbidden to free his son at the expense of someone else's life.

The Talmud, discussing a similar predicament, states, "How do you know your blood is redder? Maybe his blood is redder?" Rashi, commenting on the Talmud, elucidates: "Who knows that your blood is more precious and more dear to your Creator than the blood of someone else?" How can one weigh the value of one life against the value of another? How can one know which person is more precious? Each individual is an entire world.

This makes sense when dealing with one life versus another. But how does it explain saving one life at the expense of *millions*? Can't we say with confidence that in God's eyes millions of lives are more precious than *one*?

At the heart of this issue is how one measures the value of life.

A story is told of a rabbi and a thief who enter Heaven. The thief is singled out for his tremendous accomplishments and receives royal treatment. The rabbi is viewed as Mr. Average.

How can a thief be considered greater than a rabbi who devoted his entire life to the community, doing many acts of kindness and living an honest, decent life?

Every person is born with a unique personality and set of circumstances and a certain amount of potential for growth. Where we begin is beyond our control. However, we are responsible for where we end up and the choices we make along the way.

Perhaps the rabbi was blessed with every advantage — born to loving parents who provided him with the best schooling and a wholesome upbringing. Perhaps he possessed tremendous intelligence, compassion and a good-natured personality. Perhaps his father served as a community rabbi and he naturally chose the same calling. His true worth is not measured by how he began his life. He did not work to attain his inborn strengths (and weaknesses), and so they are not intrinsic to his true essence. They provide the backdrop for his unique challenge to strive for personal greatness. His real worth is the result of the choices he made in his effort to grow. To determine the value of his life we must take every factor and detail of his existence into account.

On the surface, the rabbi appears to be greater than the thief, perhaps even greater than many other people. But when you consider the larger framework, from his starting point in life to the potential greatness he could have reached, a different picture emerges.

This rabbi coasted through life, choosing mediocrity. With more perseverance, he could have accomplished much more.

Let's say the thief was born with tremendous disadvantages — a violent temperament, abusive parents, no money and low intelligence. None of this determines his true worth. His essence consists of the choices he made within his unique playing field.

The thief decided to build a better life for himself. He struggled to conquer his inner demons and got a job to work his way through college. When things got rough, he turned to stealing to make ends meet. But he consistently strove to be an upstanding member of society, to raise a healthy family and to make a meaningful contribution to the world.

When we compare the degrees of personal growth of the thief and the rabbi, it becomes clear that the thief is the greater individual.

Of course this example is a gross oversimplification. The complexities involved in making such a judgment are staggering — which is exactly why no human being is in the position to judge the worth of another. No one knows the challenges of another person or his potential or what the Almighty expects from him. We can never measure someone's true value. That is God's business alone. And it is never a good idea to play God.

This doesn't justify the thief's *actions*. Stealing is wrong and must result in certain consequences. We can judge the thief's actions, but not his *worth*. These two judgments are separate, the former belonging to man and the latter belonging only to God. We can't know how God views the worthiness of the thief.

Therefore, when it's millions of lives versus one ninety-year-old man, maybe that one life is more precious and dear. How can we know? The issue has nothing to do with numbers. The judgment is not ours to make, no matter how many lives are involved.

IN SUMMARY

~ In this instance taking one life saves millions of lives. Why isn't this right?

~ Only God can judge the worth of a person. No one knows someone else's challenges or his potential or what the Almighty expects from him.

~ Maybe a thief is greater in God's eyes than a respected spiritual leader.

BACKGROUND SOURCES

1. "The governor of my town ordered me to kill So-and-So. 'If not,' he says, 'I will kill you.' "

[Rabbah] answered him, "Let him slay you rather than you commit murder. Who knows that your blood is redder? Perhaps [the other person's] blood is redder."

Babylonian Talmud, Sanhedrin 74a

2. If a person destroys a life, it is as if he destroyed an entire world. If a person saves a life, it is as if he saved an entire world.

Babylonian Talmud, Sanhedrin 37a

3. All of Israel is commanded to sanctify God's great Name.… If one is forced to either transgress one of the commandments of the Torah or be killed, he should transgress and not be killed, as it says in the Torah, "…and live by them [the commandments]" — one should live by them, not die by them.

This applies to all commandments except idol worship, sexual immorality and murder. With regard to these three transgressions…one should be killed and not transgress.

Maimonides, Mishnah Torah,
The Foundations of the Torah 5:1–2

4. Rabbi Chanina bar Pappa explained: The angel appointed to oversee the conceiving of a child takes a drop [of semen] and brings it before the Holy One, blessed be He, and he says, "Master of the world, what will be with [the person who develops from] this drop? Will he be strong or weak? Wise or foolish? Rich or poor?"

The angel does not ask if he will be righteous or evil, as Rabbi Chanina explained: "Everything is in the hands of Heaven except the fear of Heaven."

Babylonian Talmud, Niddah 16b

5. Do not try to justify yourself by saying, "What shall I do? My baser drives are very strong, and they always get the best of me." This only shows that you're not really trying.

Think for a moment: did God place you in this world just to sit back and relax and enjoy yourself? No, He placed you here to…wage the battle of life on earth.

This is how you can judge yourself. If whenever your passions rise to attack you, you smite them [with] a double blow, not only do you ignore their demands but you perform a mitzvah as well. Then you know that you are among God's elite forces.

Rabbi Kalonymus Kalman Shapira,
To Heal the Soul

3

FRIENDS

SHMOOZE

FRIENDS
QUESTIONS

1. *Your best friend calls you up in the middle of the night. "Listen," he says, "I'm in Vegas and I got into a fight. Things got out of control and I killed someone. I need you to come right away."*

   What would you do?

2a. *Do you have a set of criteria for choosing friends?*

 b. *What are the most important qualities you should look for in a friend?*

1. FRIENDS WITH A MURDERER

Would you drop everything and fly to Las Vegas to stand by your friend?

Would you act differently if, instead of murder, your friend confessed to infidelity? To embezzlement? What are the limits of your commitment to a friend?

It all depends on the purpose of your friendship. If the purpose is to have someone to play tennis with, it's probably time to get a new tennis partner. But what if the person involved is truly a close and dear friend?

In Hebrew the word for "friend" is *chaver*. *Chaver* comes from the Hebrew word *chibbur*, which means "attached" or "joined." It is the inseparable bond between two people that creates lasting friendship. Do you stay friends only when your companions make wise and proper decisions? If you are a true friend, your love is unconditional and you will always be there.

Without this degree of attachment, you can't completely trust a friendship. A line has been drawn that compromises the loyalty of the relationship and weakens its foundation.

We certainly cannot condone a friend's act of murder. It's wrong, plain and simple. But what are our responsibilities to our friend? Do we abandon him at his time of greatest need? We need to be there to support him, to help him get his life back on track, to show him where he has gone wrong.

Obviously we should not go out and befriend a murderer. We need to be careful about the people we choose as friends. Nor should we stick by a psychopath who fooled us for years. Closet serial killers don't deserve our loyalty. We're discussing our commitment to close friends who have major flaws and make major mistakes. The degree of loyalty among friends determines if it will be a casual connection or a bond of blood brothers.

True friends are hard to find; it is even more difficult to be one. Having good friends begins with being a good friend. "As water reflects face to face, so the heart of man to man"

(*Proverbs 27:19*) — when we love others unconditionally and give them the quality of friendship they deeply desire, we enrich our own lives with loyal companions who will be always there for us.

IN SUMMARY

~ The foundation of friendship is loyalty and unconditional love.

~ *Chaver*, friend, comes from the Hebrew word *chibbur*, attachment, because a friend is bound to you through thick and thin.

~ Having committed friends begins with being a true friend yourself.

2. CHOOSING FRIENDS

A surgeon happens to be sitting next to you on the plane, and he seems awfully nice.

Based on this, would you pick him as your doctor?

Your cousin's brother-in-law's nephew is a lawyer. Is that a reason to have him represent you?

We do not select our doctors or lawyers haphazardly. We make sure the person fits the bill. This is the way we choose our hairdresser; it should certainly be the way we choose our friends.

Choosing a friend is serious business. You become attached to him, as the Hebrew word *chaver* signifies. If you were covered with superglue, you would be extremely careful whom you rub shoulders with. Friends have an indelible influence on your life.

The Mishnah instructs us to "*acquire* a friend for yourself"

(*Ethics of the Fathers* 1:5). The Sages are teaching us to choose our friends as carefully as we'd choose a new car. We need to have a very clear idea of what we want and know what we'll be getting before we put our money down. To choose our friends wisely, we need a set of criteria.

Our criteria depend on our goal. If we want friends to socialize with, we'll look for happening, popular people. But if we want friends to give us good advice and direction, we'll look for people with a little more depth.

What do we want from our friends?

We need friends who care about the things we care about. Would you choose a friend who says nothing when he sees you going off track? One quality to consider in our search for a friend is his commitment to truth and growth. Someone who is truly concerned about us, who will influence and inspire us for the better, is a friend worth choosing.

IN SUMMARY

~ Choose your friends as you would choose a new car — with a clear set of criteria and a test drive.

~ Choose a friend who will influence and inspire you for the better.

BACKGROUND SOURCES

1. A wise man once asked his son, "How many friends do you have?"

"One hundred," replied the son.

His father said, "Son, the Sages teach that you cannot consider someone a friend until you've tested his loyalty. Even though I'm older than you, I have managed to acquire only half a friend. How is it possible that you've already acquired one hundred? Go out and test their loyalty, and you'll see how many friends you really have."

After some time the son returned and said to his father, "You were absolutely right. Of all the friends I have, I wasn't able to find even one who would stand by me in times of trouble."

Midrash quoted in Me'am Lo'ez on Ethics of the Fathers

2. A love that is dependent upon something dissipates once that something is gone. A love that is unconditional will never cease.

Ethics of the Fathers 5:7

3. A person without a friend is like a left hand without a right.... A wise man wrote, "When I hear of the death of a friend, I feel as if I lost a limb." A true friend will love you as he loves himself.... A true friend will suffer harm for your benefit.... Friendship should endure in all its strength and never diminish for any reason. He should love you in times of poverty more than in times of wealth, in times of trouble more than in times of comfort.

Meiri on Proverbs 17:17

4. Rabbi Yehoshua ben Perachyah said: "...Acquire a friend for yourself."

Ethics of the Fathers 1:5

5. A person needs a good friend for three things: the learning of wisdom...constructive criticism...and sound advice.

Rabbeinu Yonah on Ethics of the Fathers 1:6

THINK TWICE

SHMOOZE

THINK TWICE
QUESTIONS

1. Would you consider a seventeen-year-old German in 1941 morally responsible for choosing to become a member of the Hitler Youth?

2. A fanatic and an idealist are both prepared to give their life for a cause.

   What makes them different from each other?

1. MEMBER OF HITLER YOUTH

No one is born and raised in a vacuum.

If you were born into a Shiite family in Iran, you would most likely view the State of Israel with a certain degree of animosity. If you were born into a Jewish family in Jerusalem, you would most likely view Israel as your physical and spiritual homeland.

If everyone is affected by social conditioning, how can anyone be morally responsible for his or her actions? Why should a seventeen-year-old German youth be held morally responsible for choosing to join the Hitler Youth? Wasn't he socially conditioned right from the start to dislike Jews? Was he ever exposed to any other belief system? Besides, all his friends are joining!

Yet the world does hold Nazis accountable.

Why?

Every child naturally absorbs the beliefs and values of his environment. We are all socially conditioned to think a certain way. So many of us think *our* beliefs are the right ones when, in fact, they are merely an accident of birth.

Social conditioning is not a strong, rational basis for values. Think how different your beliefs would be if you grew up in another society. Breaking out of the confines of your upbringing and reexamining the foundations of your beliefs is the first step to becoming a true thinking individual. Without questioning and verifying the validity of your ingrained values, you can never know if your positions are correct. You cannot call your opinions your own. You are just a puppet of society, an intellectual automaton.

Dr. Stanley Milgrom of Yale University ran an experiment in which participants thought they were testing the role of punishment in learning. Every time the student — who in fact was Milgrom's collaborator — made a mistake in memorizing a list of words, the *real* subject of the experiment was asked to push a button, giving increasingly strong electric shocks. (Unbeknownst to him, no actual shock was given.)

The majority of participants reached the point of knowingly administering fatal doses of electrical current, believing they may have killed the student. Yet they submitted to the authority figure telling them to proceed with the experiment rather than defy him.

Milgrom's experiment demonstrates that you don't have to be sadistic or deranged to put people into gas chambers. You can be completely normal and just not independent enough to question the morality of what you are told to do.

We are all responsible for choosing our beliefs, whether we grew up in Germany in 1941 or in North America in the new millennium. Without the strength to question authority and to defy the prevalent norms, evil is within everyone's grasp. It's just a matter of time and circumstance.

Yesterday's German youth and today's terrorists are both responsible for their actions, despite their social conditioning. Instead of actively questioning their society, they chose to remain passive.

Being a Jew means questioning your social conditioning, striving to be individuals of integrity, searching for truth. Abraham, the father of the Jewish people, became the first

Jew because he had the independence and cour.
tion his pagan surroundings. He rose above his
upbringing, going against his entire society, and ʝ
his belief in one God.

With independence as fierce as Abraham's comes the libera-
tion of the self.

IN SUMMARY

~ Everyone is conditioned by society to accept a certain set of beliefs, whether that society is Nazi Germany, Syria or Long Island.

~ Social conditioning is never a valid basis for one's convictions.

~ Everyone is morally responsible to develop independent thinking, reevaluating the foundations of his beliefs and searching for truth.

~ Without the strength to question authority and to resist prevalent norms, perpetrating evil is within everyone's ability — it's just a matter of time and circumstance.

2. FANATIC VERSUS IDEALIST

What is the difference between an idealist and a fanatic?

The word *extremist* is intrinsically relative and therefore doesn't help to clarify matters. One person's extreme is another person's center. Besides, being on the fringe of society can sometimes be good. A radical in Nazi Germany was someone who viewed Jews as equal human beings.

The fanatic and the idealist are both willing to make tremendous sacrifices for what they believe, but for completely different reasons.

A fanatic couldn't care less about the truth. He will stick to his position with a closed mind, despite a mountain of contradicting evidence. You can't talk to a fanatic because he doesn't listen to reason. He is completely self-absorbed, deaf to everything but his own ego.

An idealist is committed to his beliefs, no matter how unpopular or demanding they may be, because he genuinely believes they are true. With his passion for truth, he maintains an open mind and challenges others, not through a show of physical strength, but through the force of intellectual deliberation. You can talk to an idealist because he listens to reason and is willing to be shown that he is wrong. The idealist cares about the justice of the cause, not his own ego.

An idealist listens. A fanatic doesn't want to hear.

IN SUMMARY

~ The word *extremism* is intrinsically relative. Sometimes extremism is good.

~ A fanatic doesn't care about the truth of his cause. He is unwilling to listen to reason and is completely self-absorbed.

~ An idealist cares only about the truth and is willing to listen to reason. He is totally committed to living by his beliefs no matter how difficult it is.

BACKGROUND SOURCES

1. It is natural for a person to be influenced, in sentiment and action, by one's neighbors and associates and to observe the customs of one's society.

Maimonides, Mishnah Torah,
Laws of Character Development 6:1

2a. "...to Abram, the Hebrew [*haIvri*]."

Genesis 14:13

b. Rabbi Yehudah says [explaining the word *haIvri*]: The entire world stood on one side [*ha'ever*], and Abraham stood on the other side.

Bereishit Rabbah 42:8

3. As time passed, the honored and revered Name of God was forgotten by mankind...and was no longer known to them. All the common people...knew only the figure of wood and stone.... Even their wise men thought there was no deity other than the stars and the spheres, making figures for their sake and in their image. But the Creator of the universe was known to none....

The world continued in this fashion, until the pillar of the world, Abraham our forefather, was born.... While still an infant, his mind began to reflect.... He had no teacher.... He was submerged in Ur Kasdim among ignorant idol worshipers. His father and mother and the entire population worshiped idols, and he worshiped with them. But his mind was busily working and reflecting till he had attained the way of truth...and knew that there is One God.... He realized the whole world was in error...and began to proclaim...and to instruct the people that the entire universe has only One God.

Maimonides, Mishnah Torah, Laws of Idolatry 1:2

4. We must imagine the courage necessary for Abraham to get up and stand against his father, his whole family and indeed the entire world in order to fight for the truth of God's oneness.

We all know how difficult it is to swim against the stream of society, even in an environment that is only slightly opposed to our beliefs; how much more so for a single individual who is submerged in a society that is completely against him. What courage Abraham must have had! This is nothing other than a real stubbornness to do good, a decision not to give up under any circumstance. On account of this strength, Abraham merited to receive the covenant — a promise that will never be broken — that his children would endure forever....

Rabbi Eliyahu Dessler, Michtav MeEliyahu, vol. 2,
Discourse on Passover

5. If you are a person of intellect and understanding...you are obligated to use your faculties until you gain a clear and definite knowledge.... In order of time, instruction based on tradition must necessarily precede knowledge obtained by the exercise of reason, since learners must rely on what they are taught before they can obtain independent knowledge. Yet it would show a lack of willingness for anyone who can obtain certainty by the method of rational demonstration to rely on tradition alone. Everyone who has the requisite capacity is obligated to investigate with his reason whatever [knowledge] he can acquire and to bring evidence that deliberate judgment would support.

Rabbeinu Bachya, Duties of the Heart, Introduction

5

MARRIAGE

SHMOOZE

MARRIAGE
QUESTIONS

1. *Imagine finding the person you want to spend the rest of your life with. S/he's prepared to make a life-long commitment but not to get married, ever. Would you accept this arrangement?*

2. *What qualities are absolutely indispensable for a good marriage?*

1. LIFELONG COMMITMENT

The Torah says that through marriage **man and woman** "become one flesh."

You may have friends and relatives who are close to you. You may have children who are an extension of yourself. But your spouse actually *is* you. There is no other relationship in the world where two people, no matter how close, become one.

Becoming one means my spouse is part of me like my hand. What is my commitment to my hand? I'm not committed to my hand; I *am* my hand and my hand is me. My commitment to my hand is one I'd question only if it became infected and developed gangrene.

Certain marriages fall prey to gangrenous cycles of abuse. In such situations divorce is appropriate. But is this the case in marriages that fall into the 50 percent divorce rate we see today? Or is it that "We got tired of each other," "The excitement has gone out of the relationship," "We don't laugh anymore." If someone were to tell you he's amputating his hand because "the fun has gone out of it," you'd know he's crazy!

No one reconsiders his commitment to his hand if it's broken or ugly. No one feels his loyalties shaken if he meets someone with nicer hands. The only time one questions his commitment to his hand is if it's killing him.

The commitment of marriage is binding until it's killing you. That is what commitment is all about. No one thinks that popping the question means "Will you marry me — for a while?" It means *forever*.

Only this kind of commitment will keep you from bolting when the challenges of your marriage seem insurmountable. Only this kind of commitment will provide the security you need to allow yourself to become vulnerable and reveal your shortcomings. A good marriage requires dealing with the frustration of repeatedly facing issues, discussing problems and working them out. It means enduring the pain of confronting your evasions, bearing the responsibility of taking care of another person and learning to give in a meaningful manner. Only real commitment will prevent you from escaping the challenges of marriage. Marriage isn't always comfortable, but when effort is invested, it is always very rewarding.

The reluctance to get married is often a reluctance to make this kind of permanent commitment. We want a relationship, but with an emergency exit in sight. However, the pleasure of true intimacy cannot be achieved while having one hand on the ripcord, ready to end the relationship tomorrow.

By making the commitment to be there forever and realizing that the two of you are, in fact, one, you will have taken the first steps toward creating a very special relationship with your spouse.

IN SUMMARY

~ Commitment means forever. Through marriage, you and your spouse become "one flesh." You wouldn't consider severing the relationship unless it falls prey to gangrenous cycles of abuse.

~ Permanent commitment encourages both partners to put in the effort that leads to true intimacy in the relationship.

~ The reluctance to get married is often due to a reluctance to make a real commitment. Many of us want a relationship with an emergency exit in clear sight.

2. ESSENTIAL TRAITS

What traits are universally essential for a successful marriage?

Every good trait is beneficial to marriage, but what qualities are so crucial that a marriage can't work without them?

Consider these three: kindness, loyalty and honesty.

1. *Kindness.* Don't confuse kindness with being nice. Acting in a pleasant and socially agreeable manner is being nice. All it tells you about the person is that he or she is polite, courteous and would never spit on you. Nice behavior is not an indicator of kindness.

Kindness means being genuinely concerned with the needs of others with no ulterior motive. It means moving beyond yourself, expanding the parameters of your existence to feel another's pain and joy. It is not possible to become truly one with a selfish person. Kindness enables you to forget about yourself and connect deeply with another person.

2. *Loyalty.* Loyalty is the nuts and bolts of commitment. It's the cement of any relationship. Marriage is built on a commitment that's forever, and loyalty is the key ingredient of this commitment. With it, you can trust your partner completely. Without it, there can be no marriage — there can be only two lone travelers sharing the same quarters.

3. *Honesty.* You can't develop a relationship with someone who doesn't know his own self or who won't be honest with you. How can you achieve intimacy if you're not even sure whom you're being intimate with? Honesty is the foundation for trust and genuine communication. It allows you to build a real relationship, not a charade.

A good marriage requires these three traits. The hard part is finding a partner who has them. Even harder, and perhaps more important, is making sure *we* possess these character traits ourselves.

IN SUMMARY

Three indispensable traits for marriage:

~ Kindness: being genuinely concerned with the welfare of others. It entails much more than just being "nice."

~ Loyalty: the foundation of commitment that engenders trust and cements two people together.

~ Honesty: knowing yourself and being straight with others. It's the basis of trust and communication.

BACKGROUND SOURCES

1a. So God created the man in His own image; in the image of God He created him, male and female He created them.

Genesis 1:27

b. At first He created a single being with two faces, and then He divided him.

Rashi on Genesis 1:27

c. Rabbi Elazar said that any man who has no wife is not a complete man, for it says in the Torah, "Male and female He created them and called their name Adam [Man]."

Babylonian Talmud, Yevamot 63a

2a. Therefore a man shall leave his father and his mother and cleave to his wife, and they shall become one flesh.

Genesis 2:24

b. It seems to me that animals do not have this cleaving attachment to their female counterparts, but rather any male comes upon any female he finds. The Torah says that the human female was "bone of his bone and flesh of his flesh" and that he shall attach himself to her and she shall be in his bosom as his flesh. He shall desire that she always be with him as it was with the first man.

His progeny inherited this nature, that the males be attached to their wives, leaving their parents and indeed viewing their wives as one flesh...closer than any other blood relative.

Nachmanides on Genesis 2:24

3. We see that love and giving always come together. Is the giving a consequence of the love, or is the love a result of the giving?

We usually think it is love that causes giving, because we observe that a person showers gifts and favors upon the one he loves. But there is another side to the argument. Giving may bring about love for the same reason that a person loves what he himself has created or nurtured: he recognizes a part of himself in it. Whether it is a child he has brought into the world, an animal he has reared or a house he has built, a person is bound with love to the work of his hands....

Why do we find so often that this husband-wife affection does not seem to last? People are generally "takers," not "givers".... When demands begin, love departs.... There are some people who do not want to enter into marriage. This is because they are unable to shake themselves free of the power of taking, and even their natural instincts cannot turn them into givers, even temporarily....

In conclusion, the best relationship between husband and wife will be created when both achieve and practice the virtue of giving.

Rabbi Eliyahu Dessler, Michtav MeEliyahu,
Discourse on Lovingkindness

6

FREE WILL

SHMOOZE

FREE WILL
QUESTIONS

1a. *Do animals have free will?*

b. *What is the difference between choosing a flavor of ice cream and choosing to return a lost wallet?*

2. *Does a poor person in a Third World country have the same power of free will as a wealthy person in North America?*

1. ANIMALS AND FREE WILL

Human beings
have much in common with
animals.

They eat, breathe and sleep; we eat, breathe and sleep. A dog wakes up in the morning and decides what to eat first — his water or his Purina. A human being also wakes up and decides what to eat — some cereal or a bagel.

Humans and animals both seem to make decisions. Are we different, or is a human being just a walking, talking gorilla?

Do dogs worry about going on a diet? "My gosh," cries Fido. "I've got to control this appetite!" Do they question whether it's right to finish off the last drop of milk and not leave any for their kennel mates? Does a dog wake up in the morning plagued with existential questions like, what is my purpose in life? Does he worry about how he is making a difference with his life or if he is actualizing his potential?

We do have a lot of things in common with animals, but free will is not one of them. Choosing your favorite ice cream or what to eat for breakfast is a matter of preference, not free will. Free will is the choice between good and evil. To exercise your free will, the choice must include a moral dimension and precipitate a struggle between right and wrong.

Only mankind has the ability to discern right from wrong and to make moral judgments. It is this ability that makes human beings responsible for their actions.

When we hear news of a shark attack, we don't blame the shark. We know it's just doing what comes naturally. We don't suspect that the shark *chose* to attack out of evil intent and really could have called upon its nobler instincts and spared its victim.

But when a human being attacks, he is held accountable for his actions. He made a choice and he is responsible.

Free will is mankind's unique, crowning distinction. The Torah says that only mankind was created "in the image of God." Yet God doesn't have an image. It means that only mankind has the true freedom and independence that comes with the power of choice. In that way we resemble God, Who is completely free and independent.

The next time you encounter a moral dilemma, use your free will. You can rise above your baser instincts and ennoble your life through choosing good. We have the choice to strive to be good, not animals. This is our unique responsibility.

IN SUMMARY

~ Animals have instinct; human beings have free will. Mankind is created in God's image. Just as God is a free and independent power, so is man.

~ Free will does not mean choosing an ice cream flavor. It is the ability to choose between good and evil.

~ Free will engenders responsibility. People, not dogs, are accountable for their actions, since only people can discern between right and wrong.

2. EQUAL MEASURES

.We are all born with
a unique
set of circumstances that are beyond
our control.

Some people are born into a loving home with two caring parents and the best of everything. Others have to struggle just to stay alive.

Everyone possesses different strengths, weaknesses and potential. Some people are born with great intelligence and patience, while others are born with golden hands and a restless nature. Some are born robust and energetic, while others are frail and sickly.

But there is one thing we all have in common: the power of free will. Where we began in life was not within our control. However, we are responsible for where we end up and all the choices we make along the way. We are responsible for how we have progressed (or regressed) from our starting point.

For someone in Biafra (or any other poverty-stricken country), deciding whether to share his meager bowl of rice can be a moral choice of the same magnitude as someone in North America deciding whether to make a substantial donation to charity. The quality of struggle is equal, and the same power of free will can be harnessed by both. Free will is one of life's great equalizers. It is the defining quality of a human being, and it is shared by all, regardless of one's position in life.

IN SUMMARY

~ Though every person is born with a distinct personality and is given a unique set of circumstances, we all share the power to choose freely.

~ A person is not responsible for where he began in life, but he is responsible for how far he goes and how much of his potential is actualized.

~ The quality of struggle is the same for all individuals. Each faces his unique challenge, and the same power of free will is accessible to all.

BACKGROUND SOURCES

1a. God said, "Let us make man in our image, after our likeness...." God created the man in His own image; in the image of God He created him.

Genesis 1:26, 27

b. "After our likeness" refers to man's actions...which are done with knowledge and consciously. Man's actions are somewhat similar to those of God, Who acts with free will.

Seforno on Genesis 1:26

2. Every individual is given liberty. If he wants to turn himself toward a good path and be righteous, the power is in his hands; and if he wants to turn himself toward the path of evil, the power is in his hands.... Man is unique in the world, and there is no creature like him in this regard — that he, on his own, with his knowledge and thoughts, will know good and evil and do whatever he wants, and there is nobody who will prevent him from doing good or evil.

Maimonides, Mishnah Torah, Laws of Repentance 5:1

3. Every person can be as righteous as Moses or as evil as Je-roboam.... The Creator does not decree that a person will be good or evil. Since this is so, it is the sinner who causes his own loss.... If God were to decree that a person be good or wicked...how could He command us through the prophets, "Do this, don't do that, improve your ways!...."? And how would it be justified to exact retribution from the wicked or bestow reward upon the righteous?

Maimonides, Mishnah Torah, Laws of Repentance 5:2–3

4. Everyone has free will — at the point where truth meets falsehood.... Choice takes place at the point where the truth as the person sees it confronts the illusion produced in him by the power of falsehood.... Many of our actions may hap-pen to coincide with what is objectively right because we have been brought up that way and it does not occur to us to do otherwise, and many bad and false decisions may be taken simply because we do not realize they are bad. In such cases, no real choice has been made. Free will is exer-cised...only on the borderline between the forces of good and the forces of evil within that person....

Education plays a large part in determining one's "point of free will." A person may have been brought up to do many good actions as a matter of course. All this means is that his point of free will is at a higher level. For example, one may have been brought up...among people who devote themselves to good deeds. In this case his point of free will will not be whether or not to commit an actual sin but whether to do a mitzvah with more or less devotion.... Another may have been brought up among thieves. For him, whether or not to steal does not present any choice at all; his point of free will might be on the question of shooting his way out when discovered. For him, this may be the crucial choice; this is where the forces of good and evil are evenly balanced for him.

Education and environment cannot in any way change the essential act of free will, but only the location at which it takes place — the position of the point of free will on the moral scale. Every human being possesses the power to perceive the truth available to him at his particular level.... In this there is no difference at all whether his upbringing raised or lowered his point of free will. The ability to adopt the truth as he knows it is equal in all situations.

Rabbi Eliyahu Dessler, Michtav MeEliyahu, vol. 2,
Discourse on Free Will

7

HAPPINESS

SHMOOZE

HAPPINESS
QUESTIONS

1. If there were a pill that would induce a constant state of happiness with no dangerous side effects, would you take it?

2. What do you think is the secret to being happy? What trait is most essential for attaining happiness?

1. INDUCED PLEASURE

Imagine someone sitting for hours gazing at his framed doctorate hanging on the wall.

He basks in the pleasure of having reached this milestone, experiencing tremendous joy and fulfillment. But he can only imagine the effort involved, because all he did to receive this Ph.D. was spend two bucks in a dollar store for a cheap replica and put it up on his wall. In fact, he never even went to college. But that doesn't matter — the diploma gives him so much pleasure.

If this man were your brother, would you share in his joy or try to get him some professional help?

Satisfaction from a fake diploma is really no different from happiness induced by a magic pill. Both are rooted in fantasy. Real fulfillment comes through hard work and achievement.

Many people think the opposite of pain is pleasure. This is a mistake. The opposite of pain is no pain — which is *comfort*.

Don't confuse comfort with pleasure. Life's deep and enduring pleasures are achieved only through striving and effort, when we stretch ourselves to grow, moving beyond our comfort zone to bring out our potential. The result is a meaningful life and an inner sense of worth that enables us to feel genuinely whole.

There are no shortcuts to true fulfillment. No quick fix. Comfort is counterfeit, creating the illusion of pleasure. We may limit the pain, but we rob ourselves of real achievement and end up feeling deflated.

Facing challenges makes us feel alive. By flexing our free-will muscles we invigorate our soul and attain an authentic, unceasing sense of gratification. Don't settle for substitutes.

 IN SUMMARY

~ True fulfillment comes only through effort and challenge. There are no shortcuts.

~ Don't equate pleasure with comfort. Comfort is the absence of pain; pleasure requires struggle.

~ Pursuing comfort gives us a counterfeit, illusory sense of pleasure. We limit the pain, but rob ourselves of authentic gratification and fulfillment.

2. THE PURSUIT OF HAPPINESS

Happiness is a universal
longing,
yet so many people are unhappy.
Why?

The first problem is that we define happiness as a pursuit. It's something out there to hunt down. Perhaps we'll find it in a new car, a better job, a girlfriend or boyfriend, or a winning lottery ticket. We tell ourselves, *If only I were more confident, better looking, more successful...*then *I would happy.*

We all know people who seem to have it all and are *still* unhappy. Yet there are others who struggle with difficult circumstances and exude a sense of joy.

Happiness has nothing to do with external circumstances. Happiness depends only on internal choices.

The Sages say, "Who is rich? He who is happy with what he

has" (*Ethics of the Fathers 4:1*). All events are neutral. It is how you choose to interpret these events that determines your emotional state. No external situation can make you happy. If you choose to appreciate what you have and see the good in every situation, you will feel rich and content. If you take the good for granted, or decide to focus on the negative, you will be miserable no matter what.

The secret of happiness is to really appreciate what you have. Count your blessings every day and learn to savor the sweetness of life.

Appreciating the good doesn't mean burying your head in the sand and ignoring real problems. You don't have to be a Pollyanna. It means striving to live with joy while confronting the challenges around you. Happiness gives you the energy to accomplish and carry out your responsibilities. Worry and despair are subtle ways of not dealing with your responsibilities.

Happiness isn't a happening. It's a choice you can make right now.

IN SUMMARY

~ Happiness does not depend on external circumstances.

~ Happiness is a choice to appreciate what you have and to look for the good in every situation. How you choose to interpret events determines your emotional state.

~ The secret to happiness is to appreciate what you have. Count your blessings every day.

BACKGROUND SOURCES

1. Ben Hei Hei said: The reward is commensurate with the effort.

Ethics of the Fathers 5:26

2. Rabbi Yitzchak said: If someone tells you, "I labored, but I did not succeed," don't believe him. [If he tells you] "I haven't labored, yet I did succeed," don't believe him. [If, however, he tells you] "I have labored and did succeed," you may believe him.

Babylonian Talmud, Megillah 6b

3. He who has one hundred wants two hundred.... No one dies with even half of his desires fulfilled.

Kohelet Rabbah 1:34

4. You shall rejoice in all the good that the Almighty has given you.

Deuteronomy 26:11

5. We create the world in which we live to a great extent. While many events are beyond our control...we still have the ability to control our attitudes toward a given situation to a large degree. Hence the emotional consequences of events is largely up to us.... Happiness can be learned.... Our thoughts control our emotions, and we have the ability to control our thoughts to a great degree.... We ourselves choose to think those thoughts which promote our happiness or those with which we make ourselves miserable.

Rabbi Zelig Pliskin,
Gateway to Happiness, p. 49

6. All happiness is in the mind. He who possesses an understanding of the goodness of the world always rejoices. Life is full of intense pleasures which are available to all people, but many fail to appreciate them because of mistaken mental attitudes.

Rabbi Avigdor Miller,
Sing, You Righteous, p. 17

7. What is this epidemic disease of world proportions that robs us of all happiness in life? Our Sages have already told us the answer. It says in the Mishnah, "Jealousy, lust and status-seeking remove a person from the world." The world, as God made it, is a happy one. It is we who have removed ourselves from the world of happiness to the world of suffering with three desires. We need to run away from jealousy, lust and prestige in order to transform the world into one brimming over with happiness.

Rabbi Eliyahu Dessler, Michtav MeEliyahu,
The Pursuit of Happiness

8

SELF-RESPECT

SHMOOZE

SELF-RESPECT
QUESTIONS

At the end of one's life, no one says, "I wish I had spent more time at the office."

You'll never read in an obituary, "The deceased made over $150,000 a year, drove a Porsche and wore Armani suits. He was quite a guy."

So why do so many people spend their lives pursuing financial success while neglecting things they know are worth so much more than money?

THE HONOR TRAP

No amount of **money** can outweigh love.

Would you be willing to give up one of your children for twenty-five million dollars? What if your child would receive the best of everything but you would never see or hear from him again?

Tough call? Of course not.

If "money can't buy you love," why do so many people neglect their closest relationships while attaining financial success?

The reason is that they are after something even greater than love: the need for self-respect. Everyone needs to be able to wake up in the morning, look in the mirror and say, "Yes, I am a somebody!" As president of your own company, with a beautiful family, house and BMW in tow, you can tell yourself, "I've finally made it." For many, achieving financial success and fame is what gives them the feeling that their life has value.

In Hebrew this is called "*kavod*," honor, from the word *kaved*, which means "heavy." We give weight to the people we respect. Self-respect means you see yourself as a person of weight and substance. It's feeling that you're anything but a lightweight.

Why does success give people that sense of weight and self-importance? Not all feelings of *kavod* are the real McCoy. There's a counterfeit version out there that has nothing to do with who you really are and everything to do with who people think you are. Success may be the fool's gold of self-esteem.

Tap your finger on the table for a few seconds. No big deal, right? Now imagine standing center stage in Madison Square Garden. The place is packed. Tens of thousands have paid to watch you — the world's greatest finger-tapper! As you start tapping, your fans go wild, erupting in thunderous applause and then rising to give you a standing ovation!

How would you feel?

When eighty thousand people are cheering and saying you're the greatest, it's easy to start imagining a meaningless activity like finger-tapping is something that counts. After all, everyone else says it's important.

Don't confuse *looking* good with *being* good. Just because the world admires someone for putting a ball through a metal hoop doesn't mean that he is performing a truly meaningful act. All he's doing is tapping his finger.

If it's an external source that gives you self-esteem, you can be sure it's counterfeit. Trying to live up to society's standards is one of the most powerful contributors to a false sense of self-worth. And the standard most worshiped by Western society today is financial success.

Certainly you can use money or stardom to do many truly admirable things. But success in and of itself doesn't make you good. Genuine self-respect is completely independent of what anyone thinks of you. Only by embodying real values and striving for moral perfection do we truly become elevated and worthy of respect.

Our craving for respect is so strong, it can even lead to murder. Read the words of a ruthless mobster, who killed his best friend in cold blood, explaining why he joined the Mafia:

> *It's the greatest thing that a human being could experience. The flavor is so good. The high is so natural. When you sneeze, fifteen handkerchiefs come out. I mean, wherever you go, people can't do enough for you.... If you walk into a restaurant, they'll chase the person out of the best table and put you there. There's just so much glamour, respect and money...it's unbelievable. You're with the elite. You feel that you're so superior and that you're chosen.... I know in my heart that I would do it all again. I'm talking from the heart. So how could I say I'm sorry? If I say I'm sorry, who am I kidding? I did it and I loved it.*

> *Interview in Time Magazine, June 24, 1991*

Here's an unrepentant murderer who wakes up every morning feeling great about himself. That's how intoxicating *kavod* can be.

It's tempting to settle for the illusory feeling of self-worth social approval provides and to fall into the honor trap. It bypasses the incredibly hard work of living up to moral standards while allowing you the false sense of feeling good about yourself no matter what kind of person you really are. But in the end you become like an imposter, hollow inside.

There's nothing wrong with striving for fame and financial success. But don't mistake it for true inner worth. Integrity, values and moral courage are the things that give us weight and *kavod*. There are no shortcuts to genuine self-respect.

IN SUMMARY

⁓ For many, success feeds one of the most primary human needs: the need for self-respect. Why?

⁓ The counterfeit version of self-esteem has nothing to do with who you *really* are and everything to do with who people *think* you are.

⁓ Don't confuse *looking* good with *being* good. Just because the world admires a person for putting a ball through a metal hoop doesn't mean he is performing a truly meaningful activity.

⁓ Success doesn't make you good. Only by embodying real values and striving for moral courage do you attain genuine self-esteem.

BACKGROUND SOURCES

1. Honor drives the heart of man more than all the desires in the world. If not for [honor], a man would be content to have his minimum needs for food, clothing and shelter met. Earning a livelihood would be easy for him, and he would not have to exert himself to get rich. But he engages in this so he does not have to see himself as lower than his fellow men.

Rabbi Moshe Chaim Luzzatto, The Path of the Just, ch.11

2. A person is obligated to say, "The world was created for me" (*Babylonian Talmud, Sanhedrin* 37a). We are obligated to be aware of our own greatness. Feel proud that you are created in the image of God. Pride in the awareness of the greatness and elevation of your soul is not only proper, but it is actually an obligation. It is a binding duty to recognize your virtues and to live with this awareness.

Rabbi Avraham Grodzinski, Toras Avraham, p. 49

3. Stature flees from anyone who chases after it. Stature runs after anyone who flees from it.

Babylonian Talmud, Eruvin 13b

4. When performing a good deed in front of people, imagine you are standing in a forest surrounded only by trees and flowers. In the long run there is no difference between the two situations. Just as the trees have no awareness of what you are doing, in the long run it does not make a difference what those people thought about you for the few seconds they saw you.

Yesod V'Shoresh HaAvodah 1:10, as quoted by Rabbi Zelig Pliskin in Gateway to Happiness

5. Rabbi Elazar HaKappar said: Jealousy, desire and honor remove a person from the world.

Ethics of the Fathers 4:28

9

INTER-
MARRIAGE

SHMOOZE

INTERMARRIAGE
QUESTIONS

Do you think it's wrong for a Jew to marry a non-Jew?

Why or why not?

PIVOTAL CHOICES

The rate of intermarriage is **high** these days.

More than 50 percent of the Jews in the United States who got married in the past decade married out of their faith. Seven hundred thousand Jewish kids are being raised in other religions.

For some people, these statistics are a tragedy. For others, they merely portray a natural outcome of living in a multicultural society.

One thing is for sure — there are a number of arguments given against intermarriage that are not valid. For example: "Six million Jews died for you to be here. How can you spit on their graves?" or, in a similar vein, "It would kill Grandpa if you married a *shiksa*!"

Not exactly positive reasons to identify as a Jew. Nor are these arguments intellectually satisfying. The appeal to guilt is at best a non sequitur. The fact that my ancestors believed or practiced Judaism is not a reason I must do the same. Worse, however, than being ineffective, the guilt approach portrays Jewish commitment as a painful burden weighing against personal desire and self-interest. This isn't a strong answer to the question, "Why be Jewish?"

Another common but flawed argument against intermarriage is the need for Jewish continuity. Intermarriage threatens the survival of the Jewish nation. It is not only the end of one Jew's affiliation, but the severing of all potential offspring. If you care about the Jewish people, so the argument goes, you must marry a Jew and perpetuate the nation.

Where's the flaw in this reasoning?

The Torah *guarantees* the survival of the Jewish people regardless of intermarriage. The Jewish people are promised that they will be an eternal nation. The Torah says, "I will establish My covenant between Me and you and your descendants after you throughout their generations, an eternal covenant, to be your God and the God of your descendants after you" (*Genesis 17:7*). As a nation, God guarantees our survival unconditionally.

Even if our survival is being threatened, that is not the concern of a person on the verge of marriage. He is thinking about his own future with the person he loves. He may ask, "Why is Jewish survival so important that I should sacrifice my personal happiness?"

Intermarriage is first and foremost a personal issue. Why is it in your best interest to marry a Jew?

Sheldon falls in love with Christina. He believes he has finally found his soul mate. And Christina is a lot more together than the Jewish women Sheldon has previously dated. Why *shouldn't* they get married? What can be more important than true love?

Besides love, are there any other factors a person should consider when deciding to marry? Would you marry the person you love if he or she told you they don't want to have any children or they've decided to move to Alaska and devote their life to preserving a rare Arctic bird?

Yes, love is essential, but it's not all you need. You also need to share common life goals.

Intermarriage is so prevalent today because your typical Sheldon and Christina *do* share common life goals. For many, religion is at most a kind of cultural club you happen to be born into. Differences like gefilte fish versus mayonnaise on white bread do not pose a major threat to the stability of a marriage.

What is so valuable about Judaism that you should rule out 99 percent of the world's population as possible spouses? What is the mission of the Jewish people? What does this covenant mean, and is it something you want to be a part of? Will your choice for marriage express a commitment to the ideal of being a moral force in the world and to the Jewish vision of *tikkun olam*, perfecting the world? Or will you choose an individual's love over that goal and decide to abandon that unique mission?

The choice cannot be made in ignorance. The commitment of our ancestors isn't enough reason to live as a Jew. But our ancestors' commitment does reflect something so sustaining that many have endured the torments of anti-Semitism and felt richly repaid. There is no way to understand that commitment and its rewards without learning the meaning of the Jewish mission and studying Judaism. Appraise the treasure before selling it forever. Go learn what it means to be a Jew.

IN SUMMARY

~ There are invalid reasons not to intermarry: the appeal to guilt, which creates a negative affiliation to Judaism, and the Jewish continuity argument, which is flawed since the nation's survival is guaranteed and irrelevant to a person in love.

~ The issue of intermarriage is about finding out whether or not it's in your best interest to marry a Jew. In addition to love, a couple needs to share common life goals.

~ Does the Jew have a unique mission? What is the meaning of the Jewish covenant? Do you want to be a part of it or abandon it?

~ The choice cannot be made in ignorance. It requires learning about Judaism and the Jewish mission. Appraise the treasure before selling it forever.

BACKGROUND SOURCES

1. If one has a lot of money but does not derive any pleasure from it, it is as if the money is not his. It is merely placed beside him, for one does not attain joy from something that is not his. The same applies to Torah and mitzvot — if one does not derive great pleasure from them, this shows they do not yet truly belong to him.

Rabbi Simchah Zissel Ziv, Chachmah U'Mussar, p. 109

2a. God said to Abram, "Go for yourself from your land, from your birthplace and from your father's house to the land that I will show you. And I shall make you a great nation; I shall bless you and make your name great, and you shall be a blessing. I shall bless those who bless you, and he who curses you I shall curse; and all the families of the earth shall bless themselves by you."

Genesis 12:1–3

b. "Go for yourself" — go for your own benefit and for your own good.

Rashi on Genesis 12:1

3. In everything a person does, whether it is a worldly matter or a matter connected to the Jewish religion, one does not begin to act unless there are two motivating factors: preference and truth. The motivation of preference occurs when a person derives a positive feeling, a sense of life, a feeling of benefit, that this thing is very pleasant and sweet to him. And then there is the motivation of truth....

Rabbi Yosef Hurwitz of Novaradok,
Madreigat HaAdam, p. 122

4. "As for Me, this is My covenant with them," says God. "My spirit, which rests upon you, and My words, which I have put in your mouth, shall not depart from your mouth nor from the mouths of your children nor from the mouths of your children's children," says God, "from now and to all eternity."

Isaiah 54:10

5. I, God, have called you in righteousness and will hold your hand and keep you. And I will establish you as a covenant of the people, for a light unto the nations.

Isaiah 42:6

6. And it shall come to pass in the end of days that the mountain of God's House shall be firmly established...and many nations shall go and they shall say..., "Let Him teach us of His ways...." For out of Zion shall come forth the Torah and the word of God from Jerusalem....and they shall beat their swords into plowshares and their spears into pruning hooks; nation shall not lift up sword against nation, nor shall they learn war anymore.

Isaiah 2:2–4

10

INTOLERANCE

SHMOOZE

INTOLERANCE
QUESTIONS

1. Is it intolerant to think that your opinion is the truth and everyone else's opinion is wrong?

2. Four blind men encounter an elephant. One grabs the leg and is convinced it's a tree trunk. One holds the tail and thinks it's a whip. Another touches the elephant's trunk and decides it's a hose, while the fourth man pats the side and is sure it's a wall.

   The wise man tells them, "All of you are right."

   What is the moral of the story?

1. I'M RIGHT, YOU'RE WRONG

Is it ever acceptable to think that you have the true, correct opinion and the other guy is completely wrong?

Must we respect and tolerate *everyone's* opinion?

Searching for truth necessarily involves rejecting falsehood. At some point, one must draw conclusions. Is this intolerant? Is it intolerant to reject the notion that the earth is flat, even though there are people today who subscribe to such a belief? What about Holocaust deniers? Must we respect their views?

Intolerance is: "You're wrong! I don't have to explain why. You just are. And you're an idiot for thinking this way."

Intolerance is disparaging the person who holds a belief you disagree with. Intolerance is controlling, not understanding.

It means being unwilling to reconsider ideas and being closed to hearing other points of view. It is thinking someone is wrong for no good reason at all.

But to define tolerance as "the acceptance of all ideas regardless of their merit" would spell the end of critical thinking. It would mean we no longer discriminate about the ideas we accept. Just because someone said it doesn't mean we have to respect it. If everyone is right, then no one is right, and what's the point of thinking? It doesn't matter what I think or why I think it if I give all ideas the same measure of respect.

The world is filled with a plethora of competing values, confusing ideas and contradictory arguments. Every thinking person has the right to discard an idea if he can refute it with cogent reasoning and sufficient evidence. Likewise, with enough evidence and knowledge to substantiate our opinion, we can think we are right. It's intellectually dishonest to tolerate false ideas.

Being sure of our position doesn't give us license to ram it down anyone's throat. We must respect others, even if we don't respect their ideas. The search for truth demands openness and genuine tolerance without compromising intellectual honesty. It's important to demonstrate why you think someone is wrong with composure and care and listen to his view with an open mind, willing to be proven wrong. You're seeking understanding and truth, not the final word in an argument.

IN SUMMARY

~ Respecting everyone's opinions, regardless of merit, destroys the value of thinking. If everyone is right, it doesn't matter what you think or why you think it.

~ If you have the evidence to substantiate your opinion, you can think that your opinion is true. Similarly, you can think an opinion is wrong if you can refute it with cogent reasoning.

~ We must respect others, but not necessarily their ideas.

2. BLIND MEN & ELEPHANTS

Many people use this parable
to illustrate that
everything is relative.

After all, here are four different people, and each one comes up with a very different conclusion.

But is there an elephant?

No matter what they think, the reality is that it is an elephant. That is the objective reality, independent of anyone's opinion.

What was the mistake of the four blind men? They reached their conclusions without sufficient information. Based on an elephant's trunk alone, it's unlikely anyone will come to an accurate conclusion. What should they have done? They should have shared their impressions with each other, putting all the pieces together until a clearer picture emerged.

Some initial conclusions could have been made: this is not a piece of furniture; it's definitely a four-legged animal. Eventually the elephant's identity would have been revealed.

Isolating one part from the whole creates a distorted picture. It's like a father who walks into a room and sees his son about to hit his sister. The father punishes his son, while the daughter gets off scott-free. He didn't see the initial provocation — the daughter came up and punched her brother for no reason.

To be a judge you need to get the whole picture. The Hebrew word for truth, אמת (*emet*), contains this lesson. The word is made up of three letters, *alef*, *mem* and *tav*. These are the first, middle and last letters of the Hebrew alphabet. Truth requires seeing the beginning, the middle and the end.

Truth is complex, multifaceted and at times very difficult to grasp. But it's not relative. The truth is out there. It's objective and real. With the commitment and openness to find more and more pieces of the puzzle, we can get a clearer picture of what that truth is.

IN SUMMARY

~ There is an objective reality. The truth is out there.

~ We need to be open to adding pieces to the puzzle in our search for the whole picture.

BACKGROUND SOURCES

1. Since God is one, not two, truth is His seal, for there can only be one truth; it is impossible for there to be two.

Maharal of Prague, Netivot Olam, The Path of Truth

2. [Rabbi Yochanan] taught Resh Lakish the Torah and Mishnah and made him into a great man..... [When] Resh Lakish died, Rabbi Yochanan was plunged into deep grief [because he could not find another student like him — *Rashi*].

The Rabbis said, "Who will go to ease his mind? Let Rabbi Elazar the son of Pedas go, since his learning is very sharp." So [Rabbi Elazar] went and sat before Rabbi Yochanan.

Upon every point in learning that Rabbi Yochanan said, Rabbi Elazar remarked, "Here is support for what you just said...." Rabbi Yochanan complained, "Are you like [Resh] Lakish? Every time I would say something, Resh Lakish would give twenty-four objections! And I would give twenty-four answers and we would come away with a full understanding. But you say, 'Oh, I know something that supports you.' Don't you think I already know that what I'm saying is correct?!"

Rabbi Yochanan continued to rend his garments and weep, moaning: "Where are you [Resh] Lakish? Oh, where are you?!"

Babylonian Talmud, Baba Metzia 84a

3.   "When they [the students of Torah] speak with enemies at the gate" (*Psalms 127:5*). What is implied by the words "enemies at the gate"? Rabbi Chiya bar Abba said: It refers even to a father and his son, or a teacher and his student, who are studying Torah together in one gate. At first they become enemies of one another [through the process of debate, neither scholar willing to accept the words of the other and each one seeking to disprove the other's position — *Rashi*]. But they do not move from there until they become beloved friends.

Babylonian Talmud, Kiddushin 30b

4. Bias never obscures the truth entirely. Even after the desires of one's heart have persuaded him to accept the false way as true, he still knows in his heart of hearts that the true path is truer than the other one. He accepts falsehood as a substitute for the truth, not as truth itself.... Every human being thus has the faculty to determine in his own heart where the real truth lies.

Rabbi Eliyahu Dessler, Michtav MeEliyahu,
The Truth Perspective

11

FAITH & KNOWLEDGE

SHMOOZE

FAITH &
KNOWLEDGE
QUESTIONS

One evening Carol shares her doubts about the existence of God with her friend Steve.

Steve tells her, "Believing in God is like believing in the tooth fairy — you just have to take a leap of faith. In fact, every religion boils down to blind faith."

Do you agree with Steve's statement?

FAITH VERSUS KNOWLEDGE

Does belief in God require a leap of faith?

What does it take to believe that the Torah was given by God at Mount Sinai? Is Judaism based on faith or knowledge?

Let's define our terms.

Webster's Dictionary defines *faith* as "unquestioning belief that does not require proof or evidence." Faith is a product of desire. If you desperately want to make a quick buck, you may decide to put all your faith in a wild stock market tip that guarantees tripling your money in one month. Your mind may be saying, "Don't do it!" But if your emotional need is great, you'll ignore the evidence and go with your feelings instead. *And* you'll probably lose your money.

Knowledge, on the other hand, is defined as "an acquaintance with truth, facts or principles through study or investigation." Knowledge is based on evidence. It's rational.

Even if we haven't been to China, we *know* that the country exists, because there is an overwhelming amount of evidence. It appears on maps, it is featured in the news, and it says "Made in China" on the bottom of our coffee mugs. It's unreasonable to conclude that there is a worldwide conspiracy by map makers, manufacturers, news reporters and friends who claim to have visited China.

Of these two approaches, faith and knowledge, which would be better to base your life on?

Imagine a car mechanic telling you that you need a new carburetor and it will cost you five hundred dollars. When you ask him why, he raises his hands in the air. "You see these hands?" he says. "These are very sensitive hands. I just put my hands over the hood of the car and I *feeeel* the vibes. And, buddy, you need a new carburetor."

No one spends his hard-earned money based on the vibes of a car mechanic. We demand evidence. Facts. When deciding on an issue as critical as the existence of God, don't just follow your feelings and "vibes." Try to reach a conclusion based on rational information and evidence. Only clear knowledge can show us what is actually real, whereas feelings alone can distort reality. Faith is what one *wishes* to be true — not what is necessarily true. Knowledge is what one *knows* to be true.

Judaism tells us to build a rational basis for our belief. The first of the Ten Commandments is to *know* that there is a God. It says, "You shall know this day and return it to your heart that the Lord, He is God in the heavens above and on the earth below; there is none other" (*Deuteronomy 4:39*).

Intellectual knowledge is the foundation — but not the entire edifice — of our relationship with God. The Torah is not telling us to reduce this vibrant connection to a sterile equation. Only once a rational foundation is in place does the Torah say to "return it to your heart." We must then work on creating an intimate, deeply personal and satisfying relationship with God, assimilating what we know in our minds into our feelings.

We need to use our intellect to guide our emotions. Emotions are powerful tools, but when they are in the driver's seat, we are taken into dangerous territory. Feelings can sweep us off our feet and carry us to a world of illusion.

How much evidence does one need to believe in the existence of God? The criminal justice system provides a bench mark. After the prosecution and defense present their case, the jury weighs all the evidence and decides if the accused is guilty beyond a reasonable doubt. Not beyond a shadow of doubt, but beyond a reasonable doubt.

As mortal beings with limited capacities, we rarely reach 100 percent certainty. In fact, we make major decisions all the time without utter certainty. Faced with a decision, we strive for the most reasonable course of action. Only those who wish to base their belief on faith, as opposed to knowledge, would choose the less sensible alternative over the more reasonable option.

IN SUMMARY

~ Faith is "belief without proof," a product of desire. It expresses what one *wishes* to be true, not what is *actually* true.

~ Knowledge is based on information and evidence.

~ Knowledge is a better basis for belief since only knowledge can point to what is actually real.

~ The first of the Ten Commandments is to *know* that there is a God. Judaism tells us that our intellect should direct our emotions. When emotions lead the mind, we're in dangerous territory.

~ To base a decision on knowledge requires sufficient evidence, that is, evidence beyond a reasonable doubt. Ignoring the more reasonable option in favor of the less sensible alternative is a decision based on faith, not knowledge.

BACKGROUND SOURCES

1. The foundation of all foundations and the pillar of all wisdom is to know that there is a First Being who brought every existing thing into existence. All existing things...exist only through His true existence.

Maimonides, Mishnah Torah, The Book of Knowledge 1:1

2. Regarding the question of whether or not we have an obligation to investigate the doctrine of God's unity...anyone capable of investigating this and similar philosophical themes by rational methods is obligated to do so according to his abilities and capacity.

Anyone who neglects to inquire belongs to the class of those who fall short in wisdom and conduct.

He is like a sick man who, though he knows well the nature of his disease and its correct treatment, relies on a doctor who treats him with various remedies. He is too lazy to use his knowledge and reasoning powers to test whether or not the doctor is treating the matter correctly, even though he could easily have done so....

The Torah says, "And you shall observe and do them, for this is your wisdom and your understanding in the eyes of the nations" (*Deuteronomy* 4:6). It is impossible that other nations will admit to the greatness of our wisdom and understanding unless there are proofs and reasonable evidence of the truth of our Torah and the veracity of our belief.

> *Rabbeinu Bachya, Duties of the Heart, ch. 3,*
> *The Unity of God*

3. Only a belief that is true, and only the truth, is worthy for a person to believe. One should not believe in something that doesn't exist and think it does exist, nor should one deny something that exists and think it doesn't exist.

> *Rabbi Yosef Albo, Sefer HaIkarim 1:22*

4. Every Jew must believe and know that there exists a First Being, without beginning or end, Who brought all things into existence and continues to sustain them. This Being is God.

These things are known by the body of wisdom handed

down from the patriarchs and prophets. With the revelation at Sinai, all Israel perceived them and gained a clear grasp of their true nature. They then taught them to their children, generation after generation, until this very day. Moses had thus commanded them, "You shall not forget the things that you saw with your own eyes...and you shall make them known to your children and to your children's children" (*Deuteronomy 4:9*).

These concepts can also be verified logically by demonstrable proofs. Their veracity can be demonstrated from what we observe in nature and its phenomena. Through such scientific disciplines as physics and astronomy, certain basic principles can be derived, and on the basis of these, clear evidence for these concepts deduced.

Rabbi Moshe Chaim Luzzatto, The Way of God 1:1:1, 2

5. The Torah says, "You shall know this day and return it to your heart that the Lord is God in the heavens above and on the earth below...." "You shall know" refers to intellectual knowledge; "return it to your heart" refers to knowledge that penetrates the subconscious and so influences our actions. There is a vast empty space in the human psyche situated between intellectual knowledge and its realization in the heart. Only when a person achieves a close association of "knowledge" and "heart," with no gulf in between, will a person's actions accord with his knowledge.

Rabbi Eliyahu Dessler, Michtav MeEliyahu, vol. 3,
Torah and Mitzvot

12

GOSSIP

SHMOOZE

GOSSIP
QUESTIONS

1. An old acquaintance, who was found guilty of petty theft many years ago, is dating your friend Linda seriously. He regrets that period of his life and now holds a steady job.

   Should you tell Linda about his past?

2. Do you ever tell others disparaging information about a person just for the sake of gossiping?

   If so, why?

1. REVEALING THE PAST

Judaism prohibits one from sharing **derogatory** or potentially harmful information about another person.

It makes no difference if the harm is psychological, financial or physical. "Do not go as a gossipmonger among your people" (*Leviticus 19:16*). This applies even when the information is true.

The only time one can pass on true derogatory information is when it's for a constructive purpose, like warning someone against entering a harmful relationship or resolving an argument.

However, the following conditions must be met:

a. The information must be firsthand and not based on hearsay.

b. There is a reasonable chance that what you say will accomplish the desired result.

c. Before speaking about a person with others, you must first speak directly to that person himself.

d. The information must be accurate, without exaggeration.

e. The issue being discussed must be an objective fault, like a hereditary disease or violent tendencies.

f. Your intent in speaking must be only for a constructive purpose. If you know that you enjoy speaking badly about that person, you are not permitted to relay it.

We have a responsibility to protect others from harmful relationships, whether by alerting them to the suspected corruption of a business partner or by telling them about the abusive nature of their date. "Don't stand by while your brother's blood is shed" (*Leviticus 19:6*). If you're in a position to prevent damage, you must act.

Therefore, if your friend Linda is dating someone you know has a serious problem, you may not turn a blind eye and hope she will find out somehow. If you think it would make an objective difference for Linda to have this information, your first step is to encourage the person to divulge the information to Linda himself. If he's not willing to do so, it is your duty to tell Linda, being careful to fulfill the above conditions.

But that's not the end of the story. How should we view a person who committed a crime, like petty theft, many years ago and has since repented fully? Does he carry an objective fault today, to the point where anyone dating him must be warned?

Not really. In our case, since you know this man is a changed human being, it isn't necessary for Linda to hear this information. Telling her could damage a healthy relationship. Since there is no constructive purpose in relaying the derogatory information, doing so would not be permitted

IN SUMMARY

~ Giving derogatory information, even if true, is wrong unless it serves a constructive purpose and fulfills all the necessary conditions.

~ We must act to save others from harmful relationships.

~ People can change. It may not be necessary to reveal someone's negative past.

2. WHY GOSSIP?

"Sticks and stones may break my bones, but words will never hurt me."

Not true! Words can cause tremendous anguish and irreparable harm.

Jewish folklore tells the story of a man who slandered the town's rabbi. Later he begged the rabbi for forgiveness, wishing to make amends. The rabbi told him to cut open a feather pillow in the wind. This he did, and the feathers scattered everywhere. "Now I'm forgiven?" asked the man.

"Yes," answered the rabbi, "as soon as you go and gather all the feathers."

"But that's impossible!"

"Exactly. When we speak badly about someone, the damage

spreads and has far-reaching repercussions. It is impossible to fully repair it."

Words are powerful. They can tear apart relationships and ruin reputations, or they can build and inspire.

Just about everyone gossips, eager to share and listen to the latest dirt. *Why?* What's the allure?

The Talmud compares a gossip to a snake because both attack their victims without tangible benefit. The snake bites and poisons a human being but receives no nourishment in return. And the gossip gains nothing by destroying another's reputation.

Gossip is not just giving in to one's curiosity about the lives of others. It is an attempt to elevate ourselves. It's enticing to knock people down and instantaneously feel better about ourselves. We think we can bypass the difficult struggle in developing genuine self-esteem by overcoming our character flaws.

In the end, we lower ourselves. Like flies drawn to dirt, we ignore the good in people and focus only on their faults. We become petty and mean-spirited, looking at the world through negative, cynical eyes. We cause immeasurable pain and breed mistrust in the process.

Words have the power to bring theoretical ideas from the mind into the tangible world, creating reality. With our speech, we can either turn people into objects, stripping away their self-image, or we can elevate ourselves by affirming the good in others, showing respect and building a benevolent world.

The next time we're tempted to focus on the negative in someone else, let's channel that criticism inward and take a good long look at ourselves. True elevation comes through improving ourselves while searching for the positive in others.

IN SUMMARY

～ We derive a pernicious kind of pleasure in knocking others down in order to elevate ourselves.

～ In the end, we lower ourselves, becoming mean-spirited and negative.

～ Next time we're tempted to focus on the negative in someone, let's take a good long look at ourselves while seeing the good in others.

BACKGROUND SOURCES

1. A person shall not cause pain to his fellow man.

Leviticus 25:18

2. Death and life are in the power of the tongue.

Proverbs 18:21

3. The one who gossips stands in Syria and kills in Rome.

Jerusalem Talmud, Peah 1:1

4. Gossip kills three people: the speaker, the listener and the person being discussed.

Babylonian Talmud, Arachin 15b

5. Be very careful with gossip because with it you will embarrass yourself, for one who denigrates is merely projecting his own fault onto someone else. It's natural to take your own faults and point them out in others.

The Ways of the Righteous, The Gate of Lashon Hara

6. Who is the gossipmonger? One who carries reports and goes from one person to another saying, "So-and-so said this! And I heard such-and-such from this person!" Even if what he says is true, he destroys the world.

Far worse is *lashon hara*, evil speech. This is talking disparagingly about someone, even if one says the truth. One who actually lies is called a "slanderer."

Maimonides, Mishnah Torah,
Laws of Character Development 7:2

7. A man in the street exclaims, "Who wants to buy the elixir of life?"

Everyone crowds around him, eager to buy. The man pulls out the book of Psalms and reads, "Who is the man who yearns for life, who desires years of good fortune? Guard your tongue from speaking evil and your lips from deceitful speech" (Psalms 34:13).

The Ways of the Righteous, The Gate of Lashon Hara

8. He who has compassion toward others will be shown compassion from Above.

Babylonian Talmud , Shabbat 151b

13

WHO PAYS?

SHMOOZE

WHO PAYS?
QUESTIONS

1. Six people cram together on a couch. One of them says, "This couch can't hold us all. Maybe some of you should get up."

   "C'mon!" they answer. "We'd have to sit here for hours for it to break."

   Soon Tom squeezes in, wedging himself into the middle of the couch. Minutes later the couch collapses. Who is responsible for the damage?

2. At a roof party, a guest accidentally knocks a valuable crystal bowl off the ledge. Just before it hits the ground, another person swings at it with a baseball bat and smashes it to pieces. Who should pay?

1. THE COLLAPSED COUCH

Imagine **you're the judge,** and lawyers from both sides present their case to you.

Tom's lawyer: Our client Tom recognizes his contribution to the destruction of the couch and admits he is partially responsible. However, the damage could not have occurred without the weight of *everyone* combined. Tom's friends knew the couch was about to collapse. When Tom sat down, no one got up. Therefore all of them are equally responsible to pay for the damages.

Friends' lawyer: Tom *alone* is responsible for the damages. He should have foreseen the consequences of adding his weight to an already overloaded couch. What was he thinking? The first six people were planning on getting up before the couch would be in any real danger of breaking. They were not acting recklessly. If not for Tom, nothing would have happened. He broke the couch.

What's your verdict?

On the one hand, if not for Tom, the couch would not have collapsed as quickly as it did, and if the six friends got up as they planned, it wouldn't have collapsed. On the other hand, all six friends did add their weight to the strain on the couch. Also, they had a few critical moments after Tom sat down — *before* the couch broke — to reassess the situation and get up immediately. Who should pay?

We can find an answer in the following quote from the *Shulchan Aruch*, the Code of Jewish Law:

> Five people are sitting on a bench when another person sits down and *leans on them*, preventing them from getting up. The bench then breaks.
>
> Although the bench would have collapsed eventually even if the last man had not sat down, since the last man caused it to break sooner, only he must pay the damage. [*Emphasis added.*]
>
> *Choshen Mishpat 381:1*

In this case only the last guy must pay since he caused it to break sooner *and* made it impossible for the others to get up.

The implication is that had they been able to get up — our case exactly — everyone must share responsibility.

We must be aware of the consequences of our actions at all times. Once Tom sits down, a new situation is created that requires a reassessment and a new decision to be made. Each of the six friends, along with Tom, did have a few minutes to jump up before the couch collapsed. However, they all opted to remain seated. Therefore all are liable.

In a case where the couch breaks *immediately* after a new person sits down, even though everyone's combined weight contributes to the damage, only the last person is liable. His act triggered the damage, leaving the others no time to jump off.

IN SUMMARY

~ Perhaps Tom alone is liable. He caused the couch to break as quickly as it did, and if not for him the friends would have stood up and prevented any damage.

~ Perhaps everyone is liable since they all had a few moments to get up and instead chose to remain seated.

~ According to Jewish law, everyone is equally liable since they all had time to get up.

2. THE BROKEN BOWL

Who actually **broke** the crystal bowl?

The guy with the bat. Should he be liable? But the bowl was going to smash to pieces anyway. So isn't the person on the roof responsible for the damage?

But he knocked it over by accident.

Should both of them pay and split the damages?

How much would you pay for a crystal bowl that is flying through the air, about to be smashed to smithereens? Absolutely nothing, of course. According to Jewish law, damages are estimated by *loss of value*, not by the specific act of physical destruction. Usually the two happen simultaneously. In this case, however, the value of the bowl was destroyed the moment it fell off the roof. The person who smashed it with the bat was just shattering an already broken bowl. Therefore the guy with the bat is exempt.

Can we exempt the person on the roof since he knocked over the bowl by accident?

Jewish law holds a person responsible for any damage he causes, whether it was intentional or accidental. We must be extremely aware of every action we make, from the steps we takes to where we direct our elbows. One is exempt only in the case of a completely unavoidable accident, like rolling over in one's sleep and crushing an item someone placed beside you *after* you fell asleep.

With more care, the man on the roof could have avoided knocking over the bowl. Therefore he is liable to pay.

IN SUMMARY

~ Damages are estimated by loss of value, not by actual physical destruction. Therefore the person with the bat is exempt from paying.

~ The person who accidentally knocked the bowl off the roof is liable. Jewish law holds a human being accountable for any damage he causes, whether intentionally or accidentally, unless it was a completely unavoidable accident.

BACKGROUND SOURCES

1. Five people are sitting on a bench without breaking it. Another person sits down and it breaks. Although the bench was inevitably going to break [due to the weight of the five people] before the last person sat down, since the last person hastened the breakage, only he is liable. After all, the others could say to him, "If you didn't lean on us, we would have gotten up before it broke."

If they all sat down together, causing it to break, everyone is liable.

Maimonides, Mishnah Torah, Laws of Damages 6:15

2. If one threw a utensil off the top of a roof and someone else came along and shattered it [in midair] with a stick, he [the one who smashed it with the stick] is exempt from paying, for we say to him, "He has merely broken a broken utensil."

Babylonian Talmud, Baba Kamma 17b

3a. A human being is always *mu'ad* [i.e., he always pays in full for whatever he damages], whether he damaged something unintentionally or intentionally, whether it was while he was awake or asleep.

Babylonian Talmud, Baba Kamma 26a

  b. Can it be said that a human being's way is to damage? This refers to someone sleeping.

But can it be said that a sleeping man's way is to damage?

Since he bends and stretches [during his sleep] it is his usual behavior [to damage utensils that lay beside him].

Babylonian Talmud, Baba Kamma 4a

  c. A person is liable for damages he causes while sleeping only if the utensils he broke were beside him when he lay down to sleep. If the utensils were placed next to him after he fell asleep, he is exempt.

Tosafot on Babylonian Talmud, Baba Kamma 4a

14

GOODNESS

SHMOOZE

GOODNESS
QUESTIONS

1. *Do you think that deep down everybody wants to be good?*

2. *If you had to be in Auschwitz, would you rather be a typical Nazi guard or a prisoner?*

1. RATIONALIZATIONS

It is human nature to rationalize our immoral decisions.

Before we permit ourselves to do something wrong, we give ourselves some kind of justification.

"Everyone does it."

"He deserves this."

"It's not that bad."

"I can't control myself."

"She has no right to say/do that to me. I'll show her!"

It's a remarkable phenomenon. Why do people universally rationalize? Why don't we just say to ourselves, "I *want* to be evil and do this immoral act"?

The reason for all the justifications is that deep down everyone wants to be good. We can't do something wrong unless we first dress it up in a way that superficially satisfies our innate drive to be good. We must persuade ourselves that it's really okay.

No one wakes up in the morning and says, "What evil can I do today?" Even Hitler had the need to rationalize to himself that he was saving humanity by ridding the earth of vermin.

If we so want to be good, why do we choose to do evil? The Talmud tells us, "No person sins unless a spirit of insanity enters him." We get confused. We conveniently mistake evil for good. We get caught up in our desire for comfort and escape. We settle for illusory pleasures that in the end erode our self-respect. It's hard to make the right choices and be good.

Despite this confusion, we are still accountable for our actions. We have a moral responsibility to cut through our rationalizations and fight our baser drives.

Underneath it all, the heart beats with an eternal drive to be good. The next time someone insults you, wrongs you or just annoys you, don't excuse his behavior, but remember that he isn't so different from you. Deep down he wants to do the right thing, just like you do.

IN SUMMARY

~ People universally rationalize their choices to do wrong. There's a need to dress up immorality in a way that will superficially satisfy our inherent drive to see ourselves as moral human beings.

~ Rationalization demonstrates the innate desire to be good. Don't excuse improper behavior, but remember that the person who harms you deep down wants to be good, just like you do.

2. NAZI GUARD OR PRISONER

Surprisingly,
many people
would rather be the prisoner.

Why would a person prefer the horrors of Auschwitz and almost certain death to being a healthy Nazi guard?

Most of us believe it is better to die being good than to live but be evil. For most of us, being good and moral is more important than life itself.

There are certain things in life that are so important we are willing to give our lives for them. Knowing what those things are clarifies our priorities and brings a greater sense of meaning and weight to our existence.

This doesn't mean we should aspire to be martyrs. Judaism affirms and celebrates life. But it does point us in an important direction, telling us where we should be devoting our precious time. There are very few things in life we deem so crucial. If goodness and morality are worth dying for, they're certainly worth living for.

The next time you're confronted with a moral dilemma and find yourself tempted to do the wrong thing, realize that you'll be cheating yourself out of one of your most primal and precious yearnings: the desire to be truly and unequivocally good.

IN SUMMARY

～ Preferring to be the prisoner shows that being good is more important than life itself.

～ If being good is worth dying for, it's certainly worth living for.

～ Next time you find yourself tempted to do something wrong, realize you're only cheating yourself.

BACKGROUND SOURCES

1. My God, the soul You have placed within me is pure.

The Morning Blessings

2. God created mankind straight, but they have sought many rationalizations.

Ecclesiastes 7:29

3. No person sins unless a spirit of insanity enters him.

Babylonian Talmud, Sotah 3a

4. The evil impulse is like a fool, for it teaches a person to go along the path of evil by obscuring the consequences and the accompanying pain the sin entails, thereby dulling one's sense of shame.... Rabbi Yitzchak says the evil impulse comes initially as a guest and eventually becomes the master of the house.

Bereishit Rabbah 22:6

5. What is the essential characteristic that enables one to withstand all tests successfully ?... It is the ability to bring our baser nature under the control of our higher yearnings. It is the ability to do battle with the evil impulse and conquer it, to confront the truth in the innermost depths of the heart, to refuse to be swayed by the falsehood that pretends it is the truth.

Rabbi Eliyahu Dessler, Michtav MeEliyahu,
The Attribute of Mercy

aish.com

Judaism Online.

Spirituality · Jewish Family
Contemporary Issues · Dating
Weekly Torah Portion · Ask the Rabbi
Western Wall Camera · Jewish Holidays
Jewish Literacy · Holocaust Studies
Online Seminars · Business Ethics
Jewish History · Israel Update